45 Blackberry
Recipes for Home

By: Kelly Johnson

Table of Contents

- Blackberry and Goat Cheese Crostini
- Blackberry Biscuits
- Blackberry Cinnamon Rolls
- Blackberry and Prosciutto Pizza
- Blackberry Trifle
- Blackberry and Honey Yogurt Bowl
- Blackberry and Peach Sangria
- Blackberry Oatmeal Bars
- Blackberry and Thyme Lemonade
- Blackberry Chocolate Tart

Classic Blackberry Pie

Ingredients:

For the Pie Crust:

- 2 1/2 cups all-purpose flour
- 1 cup unsalted butter, cold and cubed
- 1 teaspoon salt
- 1 tablespoon granulated sugar
- 1/2 cup ice water

For the Blackberry Filling:

- 5 cups fresh blackberries, washed and drained
- 1 cup granulated sugar (adjust based on the sweetness of the berries)
- 1/4 cup cornstarch
- 1 tablespoon lemon juice
- 1/2 teaspoon vanilla extract
- 1/4 teaspoon cinnamon (optional)
- Pinch of salt

Instructions:

1. Prepare the Pie Crust:

- In a food processor, combine the flour, salt, and sugar. Add cold butter cubes and pulse until the mixture resembles coarse crumbs.
- Gradually add ice water and pulse just until the dough comes together. Divide the dough into two discs, wrap in plastic wrap, and refrigerate for at least 1 hour.

2. Roll out the Pie Crust:

- Preheat the oven to 375°F (190°C). Roll out one disc of dough on a floured surface to fit a 9-inch pie dish. Place the rolled-out crust into the pie dish and trim any excess dough.

3. Prepare the Blackberry Filling:

- In a large bowl, gently toss the blackberries with sugar, cornstarch, lemon juice, vanilla extract, cinnamon (if using), and a pinch of salt.

4. Assemble the Pie:

- Pour the blackberry filling into the prepared pie crust.
- Roll out the second disc of dough and either create a lattice pattern on top of the filling or cover the pie with a full crust. Trim and crimp the edges to seal.

5. Bake:

- Place the pie on a baking sheet to catch any drips. Bake in the preheated oven for 45-50 minutes or until the crust is golden brown, and the filling is bubbly.

6. Cool and Serve:

- Allow the pie to cool for at least 2 hours before slicing. This helps the filling set.
- Serve the classic blackberry pie with a scoop of vanilla ice cream if desired.

Enjoy this timeless Blackberry Pie, a perfect blend of sweet, tart, and buttery goodness!

Blackberry Jam

Ingredients:

- 4 cups fresh blackberries
- 3 cups granulated sugar
- 1 tablespoon lemon juice
- 1 packet (about 1.75 oz) fruit pectin (powdered)

Instructions:

1. Prepare Jars:

- Wash and sterilize jam jars and lids by boiling them or running them through the dishwasher.

2. Crush Blackberries:

- In a large, heavy-bottomed pot, crush the blackberries using a potato masher or the back of a spoon.

3. Cook Blackberries:

- Add the crushed blackberries, sugar, and lemon juice to the pot. Stir well to combine.
- Bring the mixture to a boil over medium-high heat, stirring frequently to dissolve the sugar.

4. Add Pectin:

- Once the mixture is boiling, add the fruit pectin, stirring constantly. Continue to boil for 1-2 minutes, or as per the instructions on the pectin packet.

5. Check Jam Consistency:

- To test the jam's consistency, place a small amount on a cold plate and let it sit for a minute. Run your finger through it – it should wrinkle and have a jam-like texture.

6. Skim Foam (Optional):

- If there's foam on the surface, skim it off using a spoon.

7. Fill Jars:

- Ladle the hot jam into the prepared jars, leaving about 1/4 inch of headspace.

8. Seal Jars:

- Wipe the jar rims with a clean, damp cloth. Place the sterilized lids on the jars and screw on the metal bands until fingertip-tight.

9. Process Jars (Optional):

- If you want to store the jam for an extended period, you can process the jars in a boiling water bath for about 10 minutes.

10. Cool and Store:

- Allow the jars to cool to room temperature. Check the lids for a proper seal – they should not pop back when pressed.
- Store the sealed jars in a cool, dark place. Refrigerate after opening.

This homemade Blackberry Jam is perfect for spreading on toast, biscuits, or using as a topping for desserts. Enjoy the delicious taste of fresh blackberries all year round!

Blackberry Smoothie

Ingredients:

- 1 cup fresh blackberries

- 1 banana, peeled and sliced
- 1/2 cup Greek yogurt
- 1/2 cup almond milk (or any milk of your choice)
- 1 tablespoon honey (optional, depending on your sweetness preference)
- Ice cubes (optional)

Instructions:

Prepare Ingredients:
- Wash the blackberries thoroughly.

Blend Ingredients:
- In a blender, combine the fresh blackberries, sliced banana, Greek yogurt, almond milk, and honey.

Blend Until Smooth:
- Blend the ingredients until smooth and creamy. If the smoothie is too thick, you can add more almond milk to reach your desired consistency.

Taste and Adjust:
- Taste the smoothie and adjust the sweetness by adding more honey if needed. Blend again to combine.

Add Ice Cubes (Optional):
- If you prefer a colder and icier smoothie, you can add a handful of ice cubes and blend until smooth.

Serve:
- Pour the blackberry smoothie into glasses.

Garnish (Optional):
- Garnish with a few whole blackberries on top for an extra touch.

Enjoy:
- Refresh yourself with this nutritious and delicious Blackberry Smoothie!

This smoothie is not only a delightful treat but also a great way to enjoy the goodness of blackberries along with the creaminess of Greek yogurt and the natural sweetness of banana. Feel free to customize the recipe by adding other favorite fruits or incorporating greens like spinach for an extra nutritional boost.

Blackberry Cobbler

Ingredients:

For the Blackberry Filling:

- 4 cups fresh blackberries
- 1 cup granulated sugar
- 1 tablespoon lemon juice
- 2 tablespoons cornstarch

For the Cobbler Topping:

- 1 cup all-purpose flour
- 1 cup granulated sugar
- 1 teaspoon baking powder
- 1/2 teaspoon salt
- 1/2 cup unsalted butter, melted
- 3/4 cup milk
- 1 teaspoon vanilla extract

Instructions:

1. Preheat Oven:

- Preheat your oven to 350°F (175°C).

2. Prepare Blackberry Filling:

- In a large bowl, gently toss the blackberries with sugar, lemon juice, and cornstarch until the berries are coated. Let the mixture sit for about 15 minutes to allow the berries to release their juices.

3. Transfer to Baking Dish:

- Transfer the blackberry mixture to a greased 9x13-inch baking dish, spreading it evenly.

4. Prepare Cobbler Topping:

- In another bowl, whisk together the flour, sugar, baking powder, and salt.
- Add melted butter, milk, and vanilla extract to the dry ingredients. Stir until just combined. The batter will be thick.

5. Add Topping to Berries:

- Drop spoonfuls of the cobbler batter over the blackberry mixture, covering it as much as possible.

6. Bake:

- Bake in the preheated oven for 45-50 minutes or until the cobbler topping is golden brown and the blackberry filling is bubbly.

7. Cool and Serve:

- Allow the blackberry cobbler to cool for a bit before serving. It can be served warm or at room temperature.

8. Optional:

- Serve with a scoop of vanilla ice cream or a dollop of whipped cream for an extra treat.

9. Enjoy:

- Enjoy this delicious homemade Blackberry Cobbler with the goodness of sweet, juicy berries and a buttery cobbler topping!

This blackberry cobbler is a delightful dessert that captures the essence of fresh blackberries in a comforting and satisfying treat.

Blackberry Muffins

Ingredients:

- 2 cups all-purpose flour
- 1 cup granulated sugar
- 1 tablespoon baking powder
- 1/2 teaspoon baking soda
- 1/4 teaspoon salt
- 1/2 cup unsalted butter, melted and cooled
- 2 large eggs
- 1 cup buttermilk
- 1 teaspoon vanilla extract
- 1 and 1/2 cups fresh blackberries

Instructions:

1. Preheat Oven:

- Preheat your oven to 375°F (190°C). Line a muffin tin with paper liners or grease the cups.

2. Mix Dry Ingredients:

- In a large bowl, whisk together the flour, sugar, baking powder, baking soda, and salt.

3. Combine Wet Ingredients:

- In a separate bowl, whisk together the melted butter, eggs, buttermilk, and vanilla extract.

4. Combine Wet and Dry Ingredients:

- Pour the wet ingredients into the dry ingredients and gently fold until just combined. Be careful not to overmix; a few lumps are okay.

5. Add Blackberries:

- Gently fold in the fresh blackberries until evenly distributed throughout the batter.

6. Fill Muffin Cups:

- Spoon the batter into the prepared muffin cups, filling each about 2/3 full.

7. Bake:

- Bake in the preheated oven for 18-20 minutes or until a toothpick inserted into the center of a muffin comes out clean or with just a few moist crumbs.

8. Cool:

- Allow the muffins to cool in the tin for a few minutes, then transfer them to a wire rack to cool completely.

9. Enjoy:

- Once cooled, enjoy these delicious homemade Blackberry Muffins with a cup of tea or coffee!

These blackberry muffins are moist, tender, and bursting with the sweet and juicy flavor of fresh blackberries. They make for a delightful breakfast or snack option.

Blackberry Cheesecake

Ingredients:

For the Crust:

- 1 and 1/2 cups graham cracker crumbs
- 1/3 cup melted butter
- 2 tablespoons granulated sugar

For the Cheesecake Filling:

- 4 packages (32 ounces) cream cheese, softened
- 1 and 1/4 cups granulated sugar
- 4 large eggs
- 1 teaspoon vanilla extract
- 1/2 cup sour cream
- 1/2 cup heavy cream

For the Blackberry Topping:

- 2 cups fresh blackberries
- 1/4 cup granulated sugar
- 1 tablespoon cornstarch
- 1 tablespoon water
- Fresh mint leaves for garnish (optional)

Instructions:

1. Preheat Oven:

- Preheat your oven to 325°F (163°C). Grease a 9-inch springform pan with butter.

2. Prepare Crust:

- In a bowl, combine graham cracker crumbs, melted butter, and sugar. Press the mixture into the bottom of the prepared springform pan to form an even crust.

3. Bake Crust:

- Bake the crust in the preheated oven for 10 minutes. Remove and let it cool while you prepare the cheesecake filling.

4. Prepare Cheesecake Filling:

- In a large mixing bowl, beat the softened cream cheese and sugar together until smooth and creamy. Add eggs one at a time, beating well after each addition. Stir in the vanilla extract, sour cream, and heavy cream until well combined.

5. Pour into Crust:

- Pour the cheesecake filling over the baked crust.

6. Bake Cheesecake:

- Bake in the preheated oven for about 60-70 minutes or until the center is set and the top is lightly browned. The center should have a slight jiggle.

7. Cool:

- Allow the cheesecake to cool in the oven with the door ajar for about 1 hour. Then, transfer it to the refrigerator and chill for at least 4 hours or overnight.

8. Prepare Blackberry Topping:

- In a saucepan, combine blackberries and sugar. Cook over medium heat until the berries release their juices and become soft. In a small bowl, mix cornstarch and water to create a slurry. Stir the slurry into the blackberry mixture and cook until the sauce thickens. Remove from heat and let it cool.

9. Garnish and Serve:

- Once the cheesecake is thoroughly chilled, pour the blackberry topping over the cheesecake. Garnish with fresh mint leaves if desired.

10. Slice and Enjoy:

- Slice the blackberry cheesecake into servings and enjoy this decadent treat!

This Blackberry Cheesecake combines the rich creaminess of classic cheesecake with the vibrant and sweet flavor of fresh blackberries for a delightful dessert experience.

Blackberry Sorbet

Ingredients:

- 4 cups fresh blackberries
- 1 cup granulated sugar
- 1 cup water
- 1 tablespoon freshly squeezed lemon juice
- 1 teaspoon lemon zest

Instructions:

1. Prepare Blackberries:

- Rinse the fresh blackberries under cold running water and pat them dry with a paper towel.

2. Make Simple Syrup:

- In a saucepan, combine sugar and water. Heat over medium heat, stirring occasionally, until the sugar completely dissolves. Remove from heat and let the simple syrup cool to room temperature.

3. Blend Blackberries:

- In a blender or food processor, puree the blackberries until smooth.

4. Strain the Puree:

- Pass the blackberry puree through a fine-mesh sieve or cheesecloth to remove seeds and pulp, extracting the smooth liquid.

5. Combine Ingredients:

- In a mixing bowl, combine the blackberry puree, simple syrup, freshly squeezed lemon juice, and lemon zest. Stir well to ensure all ingredients are thoroughly mixed.

6. Chill Mixture:

- Place the mixture in the refrigerator and let it chill for at least 2 hours to ensure it's thoroughly cold.

7. Churn in Ice Cream Maker:

- Transfer the chilled blackberry mixture to an ice cream maker and churn according to the manufacturer's instructions. This typically takes about 20-30 minutes.

8. Freeze:

- Once the sorbet reaches a slushy consistency, transfer it to a lidded container and freeze for an additional 3-4 hours or until firm.

9. Serve:

- Scoop the blackberry sorbet into bowls or cones and serve. Garnish with fresh blackberries or mint leaves if desired.

10. Enjoy:

- Enjoy the refreshing and fruity taste of homemade blackberry sorbet!

This Blackberry Sorbet is a delightful and healthier frozen treat that captures the natural sweetness of fresh blackberries. It's perfect for cooling down on a hot day or serving as a light and fruity dessert.

Blackberry Salad with Goat Cheese

Ingredients:

- 6 cups mixed salad greens (e.g., arugula, spinach, or spring mix)
- 1 cup fresh blackberries
- 1/2 cup crumbled goat cheese
- 1/4 cup sliced almonds, toasted
- 1/4 cup red onion, thinly sliced
- 1/4 cup balsamic vinaigrette dressing
- Salt and pepper, to taste

Instructions:

1. Prepare Salad Greens:

- Wash and thoroughly dry the mixed salad greens. Place them in a large salad bowl.

2. Add Blackberries:

- Gently rinse the blackberries and pat them dry. Add the fresh blackberries to the salad bowl.

3. Toss in Goat Cheese:

- Crumble the goat cheese over the salad. The creamy and tangy flavor of goat cheese pairs wonderfully with the sweetness of blackberries.

4. Toasted Almonds:

- In a dry skillet over medium heat, toast the sliced almonds until they become golden brown and fragrant. Keep an eye on them to prevent burning.

5. Add Almonds and Red Onion:

- Sprinkle the toasted almonds and thinly sliced red onion over the salad for added crunch and a touch of savory flavor.

6. Dress the Salad:

- Drizzle the balsamic vinaigrette dressing over the salad. Start with a smaller amount and add more according to your taste preferences.

7. Toss and Season:

- Gently toss the salad ingredients to coat them evenly with the dressing. Season with salt and pepper to taste.

8. Serve:

- Divide the blackberry salad among individual plates or bowls.

9. Optional Additions:

- If you like, you can customize the salad by adding grilled chicken, sliced avocado, or your favorite protein.

10. Enjoy:

- Serve the Blackberry Salad with Goat Cheese immediately and enjoy the vibrant flavors and textures.

This Blackberry Salad with Goat Cheese is a refreshing and elegant dish that combines the sweetness of fresh blackberries with the creaminess of goat cheese, creating a delightful balance of flavors. Perfect for a light lunch or as a side dish for a special meal!

Blackberry Crisp

Ingredients:

For the Filling:

- 4 cups fresh blackberries
- 1/2 cup granulated sugar
- 1 tablespoon cornstarch
- 1 tablespoon lemon juice
- Zest of 1 lemon

For the Topping:

- 1 cup old-fashioned oats
- 1/2 cup all-purpose flour
- 1/2 cup brown sugar, packed
- 1/4 teaspoon salt
- 1/2 cup unsalted butter, cold and cut into small pieces

Instructions:

1. Preheat Oven:

- Preheat your oven to 350°F (175°C).

2. Prepare Filling:

- In a large bowl, gently toss the fresh blackberries with granulated sugar, cornstarch, lemon juice, and lemon zest until the berries are evenly coated.

3. Transfer to Baking Dish:

- Transfer the blackberry mixture to a greased 9x9-inch baking dish, spreading it out evenly.

4. Make the Topping:

- In a separate bowl, combine the oats, flour, brown sugar, and salt. Add the cold, cubed butter.

5. Crumble Topping:

- Use your fingers or a pastry cutter to incorporate the butter into the dry ingredients until the mixture resembles coarse crumbs.

6. Top the Blackberries:

- Sprinkle the oat topping evenly over the blackberry filling.

7. Bake:

- Place the baking dish in the preheated oven and bake for about 40-45 minutes or until the topping is golden brown, and the blackberry filling is bubbling around the edges.

8. Cool:

- Allow the blackberry crisp to cool for a bit before serving.

9. Serve:

- Serve warm on its own or with a scoop of vanilla ice cream or a dollop of whipped cream.

10. Enjoy:

- Enjoy the deliciousness of Blackberry Crisp with its sweet and tart blackberry filling and the crunchy oat topping!

This Blackberry Crisp is a delightful dessert that highlights the natural sweetness of fresh blackberries. The crispy oat topping adds a wonderful texture to complement the juicy and flavorful filling. It's perfect for serving on a cozy evening or as a delightful treat for gatherings.

Blackberry Lemonade

Ingredients:

- 1 cup fresh blackberries
- 1 cup granulated sugar
- 1 cup water (for the blackberry syrup)
- 1 cup fresh lemon juice (about 4-6 lemons)
- 4 cups cold water (for dilution)
- Ice cubes
- Lemon slices and fresh blackberries for garnish

Instructions:

1. Make Blackberry Syrup:

- In a small saucepan, combine the blackberries, granulated sugar, and 1 cup of water. Bring the mixture to a simmer over medium heat, stirring occasionally.

2. Simmer and Strain:

- Once the mixture is simmering, reduce the heat and let it simmer for about 10 minutes. Mash the blackberries with a spoon as they cook. Remove from heat and strain the syrup through a fine-mesh sieve into a bowl. Discard the solids and let the syrup cool.

3. Squeeze Lemons:

- While the blackberry syrup is cooling, squeeze fresh lemons to get 1 cup of lemon juice.

4. Mix Lemonade:

- In a large pitcher, combine the fresh lemon juice and the cooled blackberry syrup. Stir well to mix.

5. Dilute with Water:

- Add 4 cups of cold water to the pitcher, stirring to combine. Adjust the water quantity based on your preference for sweetness and tartness.

6. Chill:

- Refrigerate the blackberry lemonade for at least 1-2 hours to chill and allow the flavors to meld.

7. Serve:

- Fill glasses with ice cubes and pour the blackberry lemonade over the ice.

8. Garnish:

- Garnish each glass with lemon slices and a few fresh blackberries.

9. Enjoy:

- Stir before sipping, and enjoy the refreshing and fruity flavor of Blackberry Lemonade!

This homemade Blackberry Lemonade is a perfect way to cool down on a hot day. The combination of sweet blackberry syrup and tangy lemon juice creates a delightful and visually appealing drink. It's a great option for parties, picnics, or just a relaxing afternoon in the sun.

Blackberry Ice Cream

Ingredients:

- 2 cups fresh blackberries
- 1 cup granulated sugar
- 1 tablespoon fresh lemon juice
- 2 cups heavy cream
- 1 cup whole milk
- 1 teaspoon vanilla extract
- Pinch of salt

Instructions:

1. Prepare Blackberry Puree:

- In a blender or food processor, blend the fresh blackberries until smooth. Strain the puree through a fine-mesh sieve to remove the seeds, collecting the smooth blackberry liquid in a bowl.

2. Make Blackberry Sauce:

- In a small saucepan, combine the blackberry puree, granulated sugar, and fresh lemon juice. Cook over medium heat, stirring constantly until the sugar dissolves and the mixture thickens slightly. Remove from heat and let it cool.

3. Mix Ice Cream Base:

- In a mixing bowl, whisk together the heavy cream, whole milk, vanilla extract, and a pinch of salt until well combined.

4. Combine with Blackberry Sauce:

- Add the cooled blackberry sauce to the ice cream base, stirring to incorporate evenly.

5. Chill:

- Cover the mixture and refrigerate for at least 4 hours or overnight to chill thoroughly.

6. Churn:

- Pour the chilled mixture into an ice cream maker and churn according to the manufacturer's instructions until it reaches a soft-serve consistency.

7. Freeze:

- Transfer the churned ice cream to a lidded container, spreading it evenly. Freeze for at least 4 hours or until firm.

8. Serve and Enjoy:

- Scoop the blackberry ice cream into bowls or cones. Garnish with fresh blackberries if desired.

9. Indulge:

- Enjoy the creamy, fruity goodness of homemade Blackberry Ice Cream!

This homemade blackberry ice cream is a delightful treat, combining the sweetness of ripe blackberries with the creaminess of a classic ice cream base. It's perfect for enjoying during warm weather or as a special dessert any time of the year.

Blackberry Scones

Ingredients:

- 2 cups all-purpose flour
- 1/3 cup granulated sugar
- 1 tablespoon baking powder
- 1/2 teaspoon salt
- 1/2 cup unsalted butter, cold and cut into small pieces
- 1 cup fresh blackberries
- 2/3 cup milk
- 1 teaspoon vanilla extract
- Zest of 1 lemon (optional)
- 1-2 tablespoons heavy cream (for brushing)
- Additional sugar for sprinkling

Instructions:

1. Preheat Oven:

- Preheat your oven to 425°F (220°C). Line a baking sheet with parchment paper.

2. Mix Dry Ingredients:

- In a large mixing bowl, whisk together the flour, sugar, baking powder, and salt.

3. Cut in Butter:

- Add the cold, diced butter to the dry ingredients. Use a pastry cutter or your fingers to work the butter into the flour until the mixture resembles coarse crumbs.

4. Add Blackberries:

- Gently fold in the fresh blackberries, being careful not to crush them.

5. Combine Wet Ingredients:

- In a separate bowl, mix together the milk, vanilla extract, and lemon zest if using.

6. Form Dough:

- Make a well in the center of the dry ingredients and pour in the wet ingredients. Stir until just combined. Do not overmix; the dough should be slightly sticky.

7. Shape and Cut:

- Turn the dough out onto a floured surface. Pat it into a circle about 1 inch thick. Using a round cutter or a sharp knife, cut out scones.

8. Brush with Cream:

- Place the scones on the prepared baking sheet. Brush the tops with heavy cream and sprinkle with sugar.

9. Bake:

- Bake for 12-15 minutes or until the tops are golden brown.

10. Cool and Enjoy:

- Allow the scones to cool on a wire rack. Serve them warm or at room temperature.

These Blackberry Scones are perfect for breakfast or a delightful afternoon tea. The burst of sweet blackberries adds a wonderful flavor to the classic scone, and the golden crust makes them irresistible!

Blackberry Margarita

Ingredients:

- 2 oz tequila
- 1 oz triple sec
- 1 oz fresh lime juice
- 1 oz blackberry simple syrup (recipe below)
- Ice
- Blackberries and lime slices for garnish

Blackberry Simple Syrup:

- 1/2 cup fresh blackberries
- 1/2 cup granulated sugar
- 1/2 cup water

Instructions:

1. Blackberry Simple Syrup:

- In a small saucepan, combine the blackberries, sugar, and water. Bring to a simmer over medium heat, mashing the blackberries with a spoon.
- Simmer for about 5-7 minutes until the sugar has dissolved, and the mixture has thickened slightly.
- Remove from heat, strain the syrup to remove seeds and pulp, and let it cool.

2. Margarita:

- In a shaker, combine tequila, triple sec, fresh lime juice, and blackberry simple syrup.
- Add ice to the shaker, close, and shake well to chill the ingredients.

3. Rim the Glass:

- Optional: Rim the glass with salt by running a lime wedge around the rim and dipping it into salt.

4. Strain and Serve:

- Strain the margarita mixture into a glass filled with ice.

5. Garnish:

- Garnish with fresh blackberries and a lime slice.

6. Enjoy:

- Stir gently and enjoy your delicious Blackberry Margarita!

This Blackberry Margarita combines the classic margarita flavors with the sweetness of blackberry, creating a vibrant and fruity cocktail that's perfect for sipping on a warm day or at your next gathering. Cheers!

Blackberry and Almond Tart

Ingredients:

For the Tart Crust:

- 1 1/2 cups all-purpose flour
- 1/2 cup almond flour
- 1/2 cup unsalted butter, cold and diced
- 1/4 cup granulated sugar
- 1/4 teaspoon salt
- 1 large egg, beaten

For the Almond Filling:

- 1 cup almond meal
- 1/2 cup granulated sugar
- 1/4 cup unsalted butter, softened
- 1 large egg
- 1 teaspoon almond extract

For the Blackberry Topping:

- 2 cups fresh blackberries, washed and dried
- 2 tablespoons blackberry jam or preserves
- Powdered sugar for dusting (optional)

Instructions:

1. Prepare the Tart Crust:

a. In a food processor, combine the all-purpose flour, almond flour, diced butter, sugar, and salt. Pulse until the mixture resembles coarse crumbs.

b. Add the beaten egg and pulse until the dough comes together.

c. Turn the dough out onto a floured surface, knead briefly, and shape it into a disk. Wrap in plastic wrap and refrigerate for at least 30 minutes.

2. Preheat the Oven:

- Preheat your oven to 375°F (190°C).

3. Roll Out and Line the Tart Pan:

a. On a floured surface, roll out the chilled dough to fit a tart pan. Press the dough into the pan, ensuring an even layer on the bottom and up the sides.

b. Trim any excess dough hanging over the edges.

4. Blind Bake the Crust:

- Line the tart crust with parchment paper and fill it with pie weights or dried beans.
- Bake in the preheated oven for about 15 minutes. Remove the weights and parchment paper and bake for an additional 5 minutes, or until the crust is lightly golden. Allow it to cool.

5. Prepare the Almond Filling:

a. In a bowl, mix together almond meal, sugar, softened butter, egg, and almond extract until well combined.

b. Spread the almond filling evenly over the cooled tart crust.

6. Bake the Tart:

- Bake the tart in the preheated oven for 20-25 minutes, or until the almond filling is set and golden brown.

7. Assemble with Blackberries:

a. Allow the tart to cool completely.

b. Gently heat the blackberry jam until it's easy to spread. Brush the cooled tart with the jam.

c. Arrange fresh blackberries on top of the tart.

8. Optional: Dust with Powdered Sugar:

- If desired, dust the tart with powdered sugar before serving.

9. Serve and Enjoy:

- Slice and serve this delicious Blackberry and Almond Tart. Enjoy!

This tart combines the nutty flavor of almonds with the sweetness of blackberries, creating a delightful dessert that's perfect for any occasion.

Blackberry Pancakes

Ingredients:

- 1 cup all-purpose flour
- 2 tablespoons granulated sugar
- 1 teaspoon baking powder
- 1/2 teaspoon baking soda
- 1/4 teaspoon salt
- 1 cup buttermilk
- 1 large egg
- 2 tablespoons unsalted butter, melted
- 1 teaspoon vanilla extract
- 1 cup fresh blackberries
- Butter or cooking spray for the pan

Instructions:

Prepare the Dry Ingredients:
- In a large bowl, whisk together the flour, sugar, baking powder, baking soda, and salt.

Prepare the Wet Ingredients:
- In another bowl, whisk together the buttermilk, egg, melted butter, and vanilla extract.

Combine Wet and Dry Ingredients:
- Pour the wet ingredients into the dry ingredients and stir until just combined. It's okay if the batter has a few lumps.

Fold in Blackberries:
- Gently fold in the fresh blackberries into the pancake batter.

Preheat the Pan:
- Preheat a griddle or non-stick skillet over medium heat. Add a small amount of butter or cooking spray to prevent sticking.

Cook the Pancakes:
- Pour 1/4 cup of batter for each pancake onto the preheated griddle. Cook until bubbles form on the surface of the pancake and the edges look set.

Flip and Cook:
- Flip the pancakes with a spatula and cook the other side until golden brown.

Serve:

- Remove the pancakes from the griddle and repeat with the remaining batter.

Optional Toppings:
- Serve the blackberry pancakes with maple syrup, additional fresh blackberries, or a dollop of whipped cream if desired.

Enjoy:
- Enjoy these delicious blackberry pancakes for breakfast or brunch!

These blackberry pancakes are a delightful way to enjoy the sweetness of fresh blackberries in a classic breakfast favorite. Adjust the toppings to your liking and savor the burst of berry flavor in every bite!

Blackberry Vinaigrette

Ingredients:

- 1 cup fresh blackberries
- 2 tablespoons balsamic vinegar
- 1 tablespoon honey
- 1/4 cup extra-virgin olive oil
- Salt and pepper to taste

Instructions:

Prepare Blackberries:
- Rinse the fresh blackberries thoroughly and pat them dry.

Blend Ingredients:
- In a blender or food processor, combine the blackberries, balsamic vinegar, honey, and a pinch of salt and pepper.

Blend Until Smooth:
- Blend the ingredients until you have a smooth puree.

Strain (Optional):
- If you prefer a smoother vinaigrette, you can strain the mixture through a fine-mesh sieve to remove seeds. This step is optional.

Emulsify with Olive Oil:
- While the blender is running, gradually drizzle in the extra-virgin olive oil. Continue blending until the vinaigrette is well emulsified.

Adjust Seasoning:
- Taste the vinaigrette and adjust the seasoning with more salt and pepper if needed.

Store:
- Transfer the blackberry vinaigrette to a glass jar or container with a tight-fitting lid.

Refrigerate:
- Refrigerate the vinaigrette for at least 30 minutes to allow the flavors to meld.

Shake Before Use:
- Before serving, give the jar a good shake to re-emulsify the vinaigrette.

Serve:
- Drizzle the blackberry vinaigrette over your favorite salads. It pairs well with mixed greens, goat cheese, nuts, and additional fresh blackberries.

Enjoy:
- Enjoy the vibrant and flavorful blackberry vinaigrette!

This homemade blackberry vinaigrette adds a burst of fruity goodness to your salads. It's a perfect way to incorporate the sweetness of blackberries into your favorite greens. Adjust the sweetness and acidity to your taste preference and elevate your salad experience.

Blackberry and Brie Grilled Cheese

Ingredients:

- 8 slices of your favorite bread (sourdough or French bread works well)
- 8 ounces Brie cheese, sliced
- 1 cup fresh blackberries
- 2 tablespoons honey
- Butter, for spreading on bread

Instructions:

Prepare Ingredients:
- Slice the Brie cheese into thin slices.
- Rinse and pat dry the fresh blackberries.

Assemble Sandwiches:
- Lay out 4 slices of bread and place slices of Brie on each.
- Add a layer of fresh blackberries on top of the Brie on each slice.
- Drizzle about half a tablespoon of honey over the blackberries on each slice.
- Top each sandwich with another slice of bread to create 4 sandwiches in total.

Butter the Bread:
- Spread a thin layer of butter on the outer side of each sandwich.

Grill the Sandwiches:
- Heat a skillet or griddle over medium heat.
- Place the sandwiches on the skillet and cook until the bread turns golden brown and the cheese is melted, about 3-4 minutes per side.

Serve Warm:
- Remove the sandwiches from the skillet and let them rest for a minute.
- Cut the sandwiches in half diagonally and serve warm.

Enjoy:
- Enjoy the gooey, melted Brie, the burst of sweetness from the blackberries, and the touch of honey in this delightful grilled cheese!

This Blackberry and Brie Grilled Cheese is a perfect blend of sweet and savory flavors. The creamy Brie, juicy blackberries, and honey create a decadent and satisfying sandwich. It's a gourmet twist on a classic grilled cheese that's sure to impress your taste buds.

Blackberry Mojito

Ingredients:

- 1/2 cup fresh blackberries
- 8-10 fresh mint leaves
- 2 tablespoons granulated sugar
- 1 lime, cut into wedges
- Ice cubes
- 2 ounces white rum
- Club soda
- Mint sprigs and blackberries for garnish

Instructions:

Muddle Blackberries and Mint:
- In a glass, muddle the fresh blackberries, mint leaves, and sugar together. Use a muddler or the back of a spoon to crush the berries and release the mint's flavor.

Squeeze Lime:
- Squeeze the juice from a lime wedge into the glass. Drop the lime wedge into the glass.

Add Ice and Rum:
- Fill the glass with ice cubes.
- Pour the white rum over the ice.

Top with Club Soda:
- Top off the glass with club soda, leaving some space at the top.

Stir:
- Gently stir the ingredients together to combine the flavors.

Garnish:
- Garnish the drink with mint sprigs and a few fresh blackberries.

Serve:
- Serve the Blackberry Mojito immediately and enjoy!

This Blackberry Mojito is a fruity and refreshing twist on the classic cocktail. The combination of sweet blackberries, aromatic mint, and zesty lime creates a delightful drink that's perfect for warm days or any occasion. Cheers!

Blackberry Balsamic Glazed Chicken

Ingredients:

- 4 boneless, skinless chicken breasts
- Salt and black pepper, to taste
- 2 tablespoons olive oil
- 1/2 cup blackberry preserves
- 2 tablespoons balsamic vinegar
- 1 tablespoon soy sauce
- 1 teaspoon Dijon mustard
- 2 cloves garlic, minced
- Fresh basil or parsley, chopped (for garnish)

Instructions:

Season Chicken:
- Season the chicken breasts with salt and black pepper.

Cook Chicken:
- In a large skillet, heat olive oil over medium-high heat. Add the chicken breasts and cook for about 6-7 minutes per side or until fully cooked and no longer pink in the center. The internal temperature should reach 165°F (74°C). Remove chicken from the skillet and set aside.

Prepare Glaze:
- In the same skillet, add blackberry preserves, balsamic vinegar, soy sauce, Dijon mustard, and minced garlic. Stir well and let it simmer for 3-5 minutes until the sauce thickens slightly.

Glaze Chicken:
- Return the cooked chicken breasts to the skillet, coating them with the blackberry balsamic glaze. Spoon the glaze over the chicken, ensuring they are well-coated.

Serve:
- Transfer the glazed chicken to a serving platter. Spoon extra glaze over the top.

Garnish:
- Garnish with chopped fresh basil or parsley.

Serve Warm:
- Serve the Blackberry Balsamic Glazed Chicken warm, and enjoy the sweet and savory flavors!

This dish combines the sweetness of blackberries with the tanginess of balsamic vinegar, creating a flavorful glaze for the chicken. It's a delicious and elegant option for a special dinner.

Blackberry Bread Pudding

Ingredients:

- 8 cups cubed bread (French or Italian works well)
- 2 cups fresh blackberries
- 1 cup granulated sugar
- 4 large eggs
- 2 cups whole milk
- 1 cup heavy cream
- 1 teaspoon vanilla extract
- 1/2 teaspoon ground cinnamon
- Pinch of salt
- Butter, for greasing the baking dish

For the Blackberry Sauce:

- 1 cup fresh blackberries
- 1/4 cup granulated sugar
- 1 tablespoon lemon juice
- 1 tablespoon water

Instructions:

Preheat Oven:
- Preheat your oven to 350°F (175°C). Grease a 9x13-inch baking dish with butter.

Prepare Bread and Blackberries:
- Place the cubed bread and blackberries in the prepared baking dish, distributing them evenly.

Make Custard Mixture:
- In a mixing bowl, whisk together the sugar, eggs, milk, heavy cream, vanilla extract, ground cinnamon, and a pinch of salt until well combined.

Pour Mixture Over Bread and Berries:
- Pour the custard mixture evenly over the bread and blackberries. Press down slightly to ensure all the bread is soaked in the mixture.

Let It Soak:
- Allow the bread to soak in the custard mixture for about 15-20 minutes.

Bake:
- Bake in the preheated oven for 45-50 minutes or until the top is golden brown, and the custard is set.

Make Blackberry Sauce:
- While the bread pudding is baking, prepare the blackberry sauce. In a saucepan, combine blackberries, sugar, lemon juice, and water. Simmer over medium heat, stirring occasionally, until the blackberries break down and the sauce thickens (about 10-15 minutes).

Serve:
- Once the bread pudding is done, remove it from the oven. Serve warm, drizzled with the blackberry sauce.

Optional:
- Optionally, you can dust the bread pudding with powdered sugar or serve with a scoop of vanilla ice cream.

Enjoy this delightful Blackberry Bread Pudding with the sweet and juicy burst of blackberries in every bite!

Blackberry Parfait

Ingredients:

- 2 cups fresh blackberries
- 1 tablespoon honey or maple syrup
- 2 cups Greek yogurt
- 1 cup granola
- Mint leaves for garnish (optional)

Instructions:

Prepare the Blackberries:
- In a bowl, gently toss the fresh blackberries with honey or maple syrup. Set aside for a few minutes to let the berries soak up the sweetness.

Assemble the Parfaits:
- In serving glasses or bowls, start by layering a spoonful of Greek yogurt at the bottom.
- Add a layer of the sweetened blackberries on top of the yogurt.
- Sprinkle a layer of granola over the blackberries.
- Repeat the layers until you reach the top of the glass, finishing with a final dollop of Greek yogurt.

Garnish:
- Garnish the top with a few extra blackberries and mint leaves for a fresh touch.

Serve:
- Serve the blackberry parfaits immediately, or refrigerate until ready to serve.

Enjoy:
- Dig in and enjoy the layers of creamy yogurt, sweet blackberries, and crunchy granola!

This Blackberry Parfait makes for a delightful and nutritious dessert or breakfast option. Feel free to customize it with your favorite nuts or seeds for added texture and flavor.

Blackberry BBQ Sauce

Ingredients:

- 2 cups fresh blackberries
- 1/2 cup ketchup
- 1/4 cup apple cider vinegar
- 1/4 cup brown sugar
- 2 tablespoons molasses
- 1 tablespoon Dijon mustard
- 1 teaspoon Worcestershire sauce
- 1 teaspoon garlic powder
- 1 teaspoon onion powder
- 1/2 teaspoon smoked paprika
- Salt and black pepper to taste

Instructions:

Prepare the Blackberries:
- In a saucepan over medium heat, combine the blackberries and cook until they start to break down, about 5-7 minutes. Mash the blackberries with a fork or potato masher.

Add Ingredients:
- Add ketchup, apple cider vinegar, brown sugar, molasses, Dijon mustard, Worcestershire sauce, garlic powder, onion powder, smoked paprika, salt, and black pepper to the mashed blackberries. Stir well to combine.

Simmer:
- Bring the mixture to a simmer, then reduce the heat to low. Let it simmer for 15-20 minutes, stirring occasionally, until the sauce thickens.

Blend (Optional):
- For a smoother sauce, you can use an immersion blender or transfer the mixture to a blender and blend until smooth. Be cautious as the mixture will be hot.

Adjust Seasoning:
- Taste the sauce and adjust the seasoning according to your preference. Add more salt, pepper, or sweetener if needed.

Cool and Store:
- Allow the BBQ sauce to cool before transferring it to a jar or airtight container. Store in the refrigerator.

Use:

- Use the blackberry BBQ sauce as a delicious and unique condiment for grilled meats, burgers, chicken, or even as a dipping sauce.

Enjoy this flavorful Blackberry BBQ Sauce that adds a sweet and tangy twist to your favorite dishes!

Blackberry Almond Cake

Ingredients:

- 1 cup unsalted butter, softened
- 1 cup granulated sugar
- 4 large eggs
- 1 teaspoon almond extract
- 1 1/2 cups all-purpose flour
- 1 1/2 teaspoons baking powder
- 1/4 teaspoon salt
- 1 cup ground almonds (almond flour)
- 1/2 cup milk
- 2 cups fresh blackberries
- Powdered sugar for dusting (optional)

Instructions:

Preheat Oven:
- Preheat your oven to 350°F (175°C). Grease and flour a 9-inch round cake pan.

Cream Butter and Sugar:
- In a large mixing bowl, cream together the softened butter and granulated sugar until light and fluffy.

Add Eggs and Almond Extract:
- Add the eggs one at a time, beating well after each addition. Stir in the almond extract.

Combine Dry Ingredients:
- In a separate bowl, whisk together the all-purpose flour, baking powder, salt, and ground almonds.

Add Dry Ingredients to Wet Ingredients:
- Gradually add the dry ingredients to the wet ingredients, alternating with the milk. Begin and end with the dry ingredients. Mix until just combined.

Fold in Blackberries:
- Gently fold in the fresh blackberries until evenly distributed throughout the batter.

Transfer to Pan:
- Pour the batter into the prepared cake pan, spreading it evenly.

Bake:

- Bake in the preheated oven for 40-45 minutes or until a toothpick inserted into the center comes out clean. The edges should be golden brown.

Cool:

- Allow the cake to cool in the pan for 10 minutes, then transfer it to a wire rack to cool completely.

Dust with Powdered Sugar (Optional):

- Once the cake has cooled, you can dust it with powdered sugar for a decorative touch.

Serve:

- Slice and serve the Blackberry Almond Cake. Enjoy it with a cup of tea or coffee!

This delightful Blackberry Almond Cake combines the nutty flavor of almonds with the sweetness of fresh blackberries, creating a delicious and moist cake. Perfect for any occasion or as a sweet treat for yourself!

Blackberry Whipped Cream

Ingredients:

- 1 cup heavy whipping cream
- 1/4 cup powdered sugar (adjust to taste)
- 1/2 teaspoon vanilla extract
- 1/2 cup fresh blackberries
- Extra blackberries for garnish (optional)

Instructions:

Chill Equipment:
- Before you begin, make sure your mixing bowl and beaters or whisk attachment are well-chilled in the refrigerator for at least 15-20 minutes. This helps the cream whip up faster.

Prepare Blackberries:
- Rinse and pat dry the fresh blackberries. Reserve a few for garnish if desired.

Whip the Cream:
- In the chilled mixing bowl, pour in the heavy whipping cream.
- Using a hand mixer or stand mixer fitted with a whisk attachment, begin whipping the cream on medium speed.
- Once the cream starts to thicken slightly, add the powdered sugar gradually while continuing to whip.
- Add the vanilla extract.
- Continue whipping until stiff peaks form. Be careful not to overwhip.

Fold in Blackberries:
- Gently fold in the fresh blackberries using a spatula. Be gentle to avoid deflating the whipped cream.

Serve:
- Transfer the Blackberry Whipped Cream to a serving bowl or use it to top your favorite desserts.

Garnish (Optional):
- If desired, garnish with a few additional fresh blackberries on top.

Enjoy:
- Serve the Blackberry Whipped Cream alongside pies, cakes, or any dessert of your choice. It's also delicious on its own!

This Blackberry Whipped Cream adds a fruity and refreshing twist to the classic whipped cream, making it a delightful accompaniment to various desserts. Enjoy!

Blackberry and Feta Salad

Ingredients:

- 4 cups mixed salad greens (e.g., spinach, arugula, and/or spring mix)
- 1 cup fresh blackberries, rinsed
- 1/2 cup crumbled feta cheese
- 1/4 cup chopped walnuts or pecans
- 1/4 cup red onion, thinly sliced
- Balsamic vinaigrette dressing
- Salt and pepper to taste

Instructions:

Prepare the Greens:
- Wash and dry the salad greens, then arrange them on a serving platter or in a salad bowl.

Add Blackberries:
- Gently scatter the fresh blackberries over the greens.

Sprinkle Feta Cheese:
- Crumble the feta cheese evenly over the salad.

Top with Nuts:
- Sprinkle the chopped nuts (walnuts or pecans) on top of the salad.

Add Red Onion:
- Scatter the thinly sliced red onion over the salad for a hint of sharpness.

Season and Dress:
- Season the salad with salt and pepper to taste.
- Drizzle your favorite balsamic vinaigrette dressing over the salad. You can use a store-bought dressing or make a simple homemade one.

Toss and Serve:
- Gently toss the salad just before serving, ensuring all the ingredients are well combined.

Serve Immediately:
- Serve the Blackberry and Feta Salad immediately as a refreshing side dish or a light lunch.

This salad combines the sweetness of fresh blackberries with the salty tanginess of feta cheese, creating a delicious harmony of flavors. The addition of nuts provides a delightful crunch, and the balsamic vinaigrette ties everything together. Enjoy!

Blackberry Galette

Ingredients:

For the Dough:

- 1 1/4 cups all-purpose flour
- 1/2 teaspoon granulated sugar
- 1/4 teaspoon salt
- 1/2 cup unsalted butter, cold and cut into small cubes
- 3-4 tablespoons ice water

For the Filling:

- 3 cups fresh blackberries, rinsed and drained
- 1/2 cup granulated sugar (adjust according to sweetness of berries)
- 2 tablespoons cornstarch
- 1 tablespoon lemon juice
- Zest of one lemon

For Assembly:

- 1 tablespoon milk or cream (for brushing the crust)
- 1-2 tablespoons turbinado sugar (for sprinkling)

Instructions:

1. Prepare the Dough:

- In a food processor, combine the flour, sugar, and salt. Pulse to mix.
- Add the cold butter cubes and pulse until the mixture resembles coarse crumbs.
- Gradually add the ice water, one tablespoon at a time, and pulse until the dough just comes together.
- Turn the dough out onto a floured surface, shape it into a disk, wrap it in plastic wrap, and refrigerate for at least 30 minutes.

2. Preheat the Oven:

- Preheat your oven to 375°F (190°C). Line a baking sheet with parchment paper.

3. Prepare the Filling:

- In a bowl, gently toss the blackberries with sugar, cornstarch, lemon juice, and lemon zest. Let it sit for a few minutes to allow the berries to release some juices.

4. Roll out the Dough:

- On a floured surface, roll out the chilled dough into a circle about 12 inches in diameter.

5. Assemble the Galette:

- Transfer the rolled-out dough to the prepared baking sheet.
- Spoon the blackberry filling onto the center of the dough, leaving a border around the edges.

6. Fold and Seal:

- Carefully fold the edges of the dough over the filling, creating pleats as you go.
- Press down lightly to seal the edges.

7. Brush with Milk and Sugar:

- Brush the exposed edges of the dough with milk or cream.
- Sprinkle turbinado sugar over the edges for a sweet, crunchy finish.

8. Bake:

- Bake in the preheated oven for about 35-40 minutes or until the crust is golden brown and the filling is bubbly.

9. Cool and Serve:

- Allow the galette to cool on the baking sheet for a few minutes, then transfer it to a wire rack to cool completely.

10. Enjoy:

- Slice and serve your delicious Blackberry Galette on its own or with a scoop of vanilla ice cream.

This rustic blackberry galette is a wonderful way to showcase the sweetness of fresh blackberries in a simple, free-form pastry. The golden, flaky crust and juicy berry filling make it a delightful treat. Enjoy!

Blackberry Breakfast Bars

Ingredients:

For the Crust and Crumble:

- 1 1/2 cups old-fashioned oats
- 1 1/2 cups all-purpose flour
- 1 cup brown sugar, packed
- 1/2 teaspoon baking powder
- 1/4 teaspoon salt
- 1 cup unsalted butter, cold and cut into small cubes

For the Blackberry Filling:

- 3 cups fresh blackberries, rinsed and drained
- 1/2 cup granulated sugar
- 2 tablespoons cornstarch
- 1 tablespoon lemon juice
- Zest of one lemon

Instructions:

1. Preheat the Oven:

- Preheat your oven to 350°F (175°C). Grease or line a 9x13-inch baking pan with parchment paper.

2. Make the Crust and Crumble:

- In a large bowl, combine the oats, flour, brown sugar, baking powder, and salt.
- Add the cold, cubed butter and use your fingers or a pastry cutter to incorporate it into the dry ingredients until the mixture resembles coarse crumbs.

3. Reserve Some Mixture:

- Set aside about 1 1/2 cups of the crumb mixture to use as the topping.

4. Press the Crust:

- Press the remaining crumb mixture into the bottom of the prepared baking pan to create a crust.

5. Prepare the Blackberry Filling:

- In a bowl, gently toss the blackberries with sugar, cornstarch, lemon juice, and lemon zest.

6. Add the Filling:

- Evenly spread the blackberry mixture over the crust in the baking pan.

7. Add the Crumble Topping:

- Sprinkle the reserved crumb mixture evenly over the blackberry filling.

8. Bake:

- Bake in the preheated oven for about 40-45 minutes or until the top is golden brown, and the blackberry filling is bubbly.

9. Cool and Slice:

- Allow the bars to cool completely in the pan before slicing into squares.

10. Enjoy:

- Once cooled, cut into squares and enjoy these delicious Blackberry Breakfast Bars with a cup of coffee or tea!

These breakfast bars are a delightful combination of a buttery oat crust, sweet blackberry filling, and a crumbly topping. They make for a tasty and portable breakfast or snack. Enjoy!

Blackberry Basil Lemonade

Ingredients:

- 1 cup fresh blackberries
- 1/2 cup fresh basil leaves
- 1 cup granulated sugar
- 1 cup water
- 1 cup freshly squeezed lemon juice (about 4-5 lemons)
- 4 cups cold water
- Ice cubes
- Fresh blackberries and basil leaves for garnish

Instructions:

1. Make Simple Syrup:

- In a small saucepan, combine the blackberries, basil leaves, sugar, and 1 cup of water. Bring to a simmer over medium heat, stirring occasionally, until the sugar has completely dissolved, and the blackberries have released their juices.

2. Strain and Cool:

- Strain the blackberry basil mixture through a fine-mesh sieve into a bowl, pressing on the solids to extract as much liquid as possible. Discard the solids and let the blackberry basil simple syrup cool.

3. Prepare Lemonade Base:

- In a large pitcher, combine the freshly squeezed lemon juice and 4 cups of cold water.

4. Mix Blackberry Basil Syrup:

- Add the cooled blackberry basil simple syrup to the lemonade base. Stir well to combine.

5. Chill:

- Place the pitcher in the refrigerator to chill for at least 1-2 hours to allow the flavors to meld.

6. Serve:

- Fill glasses with ice cubes and pour the blackberry basil lemonade over the ice.

7. Garnish:

- Garnish each glass with a few fresh blackberries and a basil leaf.

8. Enjoy:

- Stir and enjoy this refreshing Blackberry Basil Lemonade on a hot day!

This blackberry basil lemonade combines the sweetness of blackberries, the herbal notes of basil, and the tartness of lemons for a delightful and unique twist on classic lemonade. It's a perfect way to cool down and enjoy the flavors of summer.

Blackberry and Spinach Salad

Ingredients:

For the Salad:

- 6 cups fresh baby spinach leaves, washed and dried
- 1 cup fresh blackberries, washed
- 1/2 cup crumbled feta cheese
- 1/4 cup red onion, thinly sliced
- 1/4 cup sliced almonds, toasted

For the Dressing:

- 3 tablespoons balsamic vinegar
- 2 tablespoons extra-virgin olive oil
- 1 tablespoon honey
- 1 teaspoon Dijon mustard
- Salt and pepper to taste

Instructions:

1. Prepare the Salad:

- In a large salad bowl, combine the fresh baby spinach, blackberries, crumbled feta cheese, sliced red onion, and toasted sliced almonds.

2. Make the Dressing:

- In a small bowl, whisk together the balsamic vinegar, extra-virgin olive oil, honey, Dijon mustard, salt, and pepper until well combined.

3. Toss the Salad:

- Drizzle the dressing over the salad ingredients.

4. Toss Well:

- Gently toss the salad to ensure all ingredients are evenly coated with the dressing.

5. Serve:

- Divide the salad among serving plates.

6. Garnish:

- If desired, garnish with additional blackberries, feta cheese, and sliced almonds.

7. Enjoy:

- Serve immediately and enjoy this refreshing and flavorful Blackberry and Spinach Salad!

This salad combines the freshness of baby spinach with the sweetness of blackberries, the creaminess of feta cheese, and the crunch of toasted almonds. The balsamic vinaigrette adds a tangy and slightly sweet flavor, making it a perfect side dish or a light meal on its own.

Blackberry Barbecue Ribs

Ingredients:

For the Ribs:

- 2 racks of baby back ribs
- Salt and pepper, to taste
- 1 tablespoon smoked paprika
- 1 tablespoon garlic powder
- 1 tablespoon onion powder
- 1 teaspoon cayenne pepper (adjust to taste)

For the Blackberry Barbecue Sauce:

- 1 cup fresh blackberries
- 1/2 cup ketchup
- 1/4 cup apple cider vinegar
- 2 tablespoons brown sugar
- 1 tablespoon Worcestershire sauce
- 1 teaspoon Dijon mustard
- Salt and pepper, to taste

Instructions:

1. Preheat the Oven:

- Preheat your oven to 300°F (150°C).

2. Prepare the Ribs:

- Remove the membrane from the back of the ribs. Season both sides of the ribs with salt, pepper, smoked paprika, garlic powder, onion powder, and cayenne pepper.

3. Wrap and Bake:

- Wrap each rack of ribs tightly in aluminum foil. Place them on a baking sheet and bake in the preheated oven for 2.5 to 3 hours or until the ribs are tender.

4. Make the Blackberry Barbecue Sauce:

- In a saucepan, combine fresh blackberries, ketchup, apple cider vinegar, brown sugar, Worcestershire sauce, Dijon mustard, salt, and pepper.

5. Simmer:

- Bring the sauce to a simmer over medium heat. Use a spoon to mash the blackberries and stir the mixture until it thickens slightly. Adjust the seasoning to taste.

6. Grill the Ribs:

- Preheat your grill to medium-high heat.
- Unwrap the ribs and place them on the grill. Brush a generous amount of the blackberry barbecue sauce on both sides of the ribs.
- Grill the ribs for about 10-15 minutes, turning and basting with more sauce until they are nicely glazed and have grill marks.

7. Rest and Serve:

- Let the ribs rest for a few minutes before slicing between the bones.

8. Serve:

- Serve the blackberry barbecue ribs with extra sauce on the side.

9. Enjoy:

- Enjoy these flavorful and juicy Blackberry Barbecue Ribs!

The combination of sweet blackberries and tangy barbecue sauce adds a unique twist to classic barbecue ribs, making them a delicious and crowd-pleasing dish.

Blackberry and Ricotta Toast

Ingredients:

- Sliced bread (whole grain or your choice)
- Fresh blackberries
- Ricotta cheese
- Honey
- Fresh mint leaves (optional)

Instructions:

1. Toast the Bread:

- Toast slices of bread until they reach your desired level of crispiness.

2. Spread Ricotta:

- Spread a generous layer of ricotta cheese on each slice of toasted bread.

3. Add Blackberries:

- Place fresh blackberries on top of the ricotta layer. You can cut the blackberries in half or leave them whole, depending on your preference.

4. Drizzle with Honey:

- Drizzle honey over the blackberries and ricotta. The sweetness of honey complements the tartness of the blackberries and the creaminess of the ricotta.

5. Garnish with Mint (Optional):

- For an extra burst of freshness, garnish the toasts with fresh mint leaves. Mint adds a lovely aroma and flavor to the dish.

6. Serve:

- Arrange the Blackberry and Ricotta Toasts on a plate and serve immediately.

7. Enjoy:

- Enjoy these delightful toasts as a quick and tasty breakfast, brunch, or snack.

This Blackberry and Ricotta Toast is a delightful combination of creamy ricotta, juicy blackberries, and the natural sweetness of honey. It's a versatile recipe that allows you to customize the toppings and enjoy a delicious and visually appealing dish.

Blackberry Crumble Bars

Ingredients:

For the Crust and Crumble:

- 1 1/2 cups all-purpose flour
- 1/2 cup granulated sugar
- 1/4 teaspoon salt
- 1/2 cup unsalted butter, cold and cut into small pieces
- 1 teaspoon vanilla extract

For the Blackberry Filling:

- 2 cups fresh blackberries
- 1/4 cup granulated sugar
- 2 tablespoons lemon juice
- 1 tablespoon cornstarch

Instructions:

1. Preheat the Oven:

- Preheat your oven to 350°F (175°C). Grease or line a baking pan with parchment paper.

2. Make the Crust and Crumble:

- In a large mixing bowl, combine the flour, sugar, and salt.
- Add the cold, cubed butter to the flour mixture. Use a pastry cutter or your hands to cut the butter into the dry ingredients until the mixture resembles coarse crumbs.
- Add the vanilla extract and mix until combined.
- Reserve about 1 cup of the mixture for the crumble topping. Press the remaining mixture into the bottom of the prepared baking pan to form the crust.

3. Prepare the Blackberry Filling:

- In a separate bowl, gently toss the blackberries with sugar, lemon juice, and cornstarch until the berries are coated.

4. Assemble the Bars:

- Spread the blackberry filling evenly over the crust in the baking pan.
- Sprinkle the reserved crumb mixture over the blackberry layer to create the crumble topping.

5. Bake:

- Bake in the preheated oven for 40-45 minutes or until the top is golden brown and the blackberry filling is bubbly.

6. Cool and Cut:

- Allow the bars to cool completely in the pan. Once cooled, refrigerate for at least an hour to help set the bars.
- Once chilled, lift the bars out of the pan using the parchment paper and place them on a cutting board.
- Cut into squares or bars.

7. Serve:

- Serve the Blackberry Crumble Bars at room temperature and enjoy!

These bars are a delightful combination of buttery crust, sweet blackberry filling, and a crumbly topping. They make a perfect treat for dessert, snack, or brunch.

Blackberry Glazed Salmon

Ingredients:

- 4 salmon fillets
- Salt and black pepper, to taste
- 1 cup fresh blackberries
- 2 tablespoons balsamic vinegar
- 2 tablespoons honey
- 1 tablespoon Dijon mustard
- 2 cloves garlic, minced
- 1 tablespoon olive oil
- Fresh parsley, chopped (for garnish)

Instructions:

1. Prepare the Salmon:

- Season the salmon fillets with salt and black pepper on both sides.

2. Make the Blackberry Glaze:

- In a blender or food processor, combine the blackberries, balsamic vinegar, honey, Dijon mustard, and minced garlic. Blend until smooth.
- Strain the blackberry mixture through a fine-mesh sieve into a bowl to remove seeds. You should have a smooth glaze.

3. Cook the Salmon:

- In a skillet over medium-high heat, heat olive oil. Place the seasoned salmon fillets in the skillet, skin side down.
- Cook the salmon for about 3-4 minutes on each side, or until it reaches your desired level of doneness.

4. Glaze the Salmon:

- Once the salmon is almost cooked, pour the blackberry glaze over the fillets.

- Allow the glaze to simmer and coat the salmon for an additional 2-3 minutes, or until the salmon is fully cooked and the glaze has thickened.

5. Serve:

- Transfer the glazed salmon fillets to serving plates.
- Drizzle any remaining glaze over the top.
- Garnish with chopped fresh parsley.

6. Enjoy:

- Serve the Blackberry Glazed Salmon immediately and enjoy this flavorful and elegant dish!

The combination of sweet blackberry glaze with the savory salmon creates a deliciously unique flavor profile. It's a perfect dish for a special dinner or when you want to impress with a gourmet touch.

Blackberry and Mint Sorbet

Ingredients:

- 3 cups fresh blackberries
- 1 cup granulated sugar
- 1 cup water
- Juice of 2 lemons
- Zest of 1 lemon
- 1/4 cup fresh mint leaves, finely chopped

Instructions:

1. Prepare the Blackberries:

- Rinse the blackberries under cold water and remove any stems.

2. Make Simple Syrup:

- In a saucepan, combine the sugar and water. Heat over medium heat, stirring occasionally, until the sugar dissolves completely. Allow the mixture to cool.

3. Blend Blackberries:

- In a blender or food processor, blend the fresh blackberries until smooth.

4. Strain the Blackberry Puree:

- Strain the blackberry puree through a fine-mesh sieve into a bowl to remove seeds. Press the mixture with a spatula to extract as much liquid as possible.

5. Mix Ingredients:

- In a mixing bowl, combine the strained blackberry puree, simple syrup, lemon juice, lemon zest, and chopped mint. Stir well to combine.

6. Chill the Mixture:

- Refrigerate the mixture for at least 2 hours or until it's thoroughly chilled.

7. Churn the Sorbet:

- Pour the chilled mixture into an ice cream maker and churn according to the manufacturer's instructions.

8. Freeze:

- Transfer the churned sorbet into a lidded container and freeze for an additional 3-4 hours or until firm.

9. Serve:

- Scoop the Blackberry and Mint Sorbet into bowls or cones.

10. Garnish and Enjoy:

- Garnish with fresh mint leaves if desired.
- Enjoy the refreshing and flavorful Blackberry and Mint Sorbet!

This sorbet is a delightful and cooling treat, perfect for a hot day or as a light dessert option. The combination of blackberries and fresh mint adds a burst of fruity and herbal flavors.

Blackberry Popsicles

Ingredients:

- 2 cups fresh blackberries
- 1/4 cup honey or maple syrup (adjust according to sweetness preference)
- 1 tablespoon fresh lemon juice
- 1/2 cup water

Instructions:

1. Prepare Blackberries:

- Rinse the blackberries under cold water and remove any stems.

2. Blend Ingredients:

- In a blender, combine the blackberries, honey or maple syrup, fresh lemon juice, and water. Blend until smooth.

3. Strain (Optional):

- If you prefer a smoother texture, you can strain the mixture through a fine-mesh sieve to remove seeds. Press the mixture with a spatula to extract as much liquid as possible.

4. Fill Popsicle Molds:

- Pour the blackberry mixture into popsicle molds.

5. Insert Sticks:

- Insert popsicle sticks into the molds. If your molds have lids, place them on top.

6. Freeze:

- Place the popsicle molds in the freezer and let them freeze for at least 4-6 hours or until completely solid.

7. Unmold and Enjoy:

- Once the blackberry popsicles are frozen, run the molds under warm water for a few seconds to loosen the popsicles.
- Gently pull the popsicles out of the molds.

8. Serve and Enjoy:

- Serve these refreshing Blackberry Popsicles on a hot day or whenever you're in the mood for a fruity frozen treat.

Feel free to customize the sweetness level by adjusting the amount of honey or maple syrup according to your taste. Enjoy!

Blackberry and Goat Cheese Crostini

Ingredients:

- Baguette, sliced into 1/2-inch rounds
- Olive oil
- 1 cup fresh blackberries
- 1 tablespoon balsamic vinegar
- 1 teaspoon honey
- 4 ounces goat cheese
- Fresh thyme leaves (for garnish)
- Salt and black pepper (to taste)

Instructions:

1. Toast the Baguette:

- Preheat your oven to 375°F (190°C).
- Place the baguette slices on a baking sheet and brush each slice with olive oil.
- Toast in the oven for about 8-10 minutes or until the edges are golden and crispy.

2. Prepare Blackberry Compote:

- In a small saucepan, combine the blackberries, balsamic vinegar, and honey.
- Cook over medium heat, stirring occasionally, until the blackberries break down and the mixture thickens slightly (about 5-7 minutes).
- Remove from heat and let it cool.

3. Assemble Crostini:

- Spread a layer of goat cheese on each toasted baguette slice.

4. Add Blackberry Compote:

- Spoon a small amount of the blackberry compote over the goat cheese on each crostini.

5. Season and Garnish:

- Sprinkle a pinch of salt and black pepper over the crostini.

- Garnish with fresh thyme leaves for added flavor.

6. Serve:

- Arrange the Blackberry and Goat Cheese Crostini on a serving platter and serve immediately.

These crostini are a delightful combination of sweet, savory, and tangy flavors. They make a great appetizer for gatherings or a tasty snack for any occasion. Enjoy!

Blackberry Biscuits

Ingredients:

For the Biscuits:

- 2 cups all-purpose flour
- 1 tablespoon baking powder
- 1/2 teaspoon baking soda
- 1/2 teaspoon salt
- 1/4 cup granulated sugar
- 1/2 cup unsalted butter, cold and cut into small pieces
- 3/4 cup buttermilk
- 1 teaspoon vanilla extract

For the Blackberry Filling:

- 1 cup fresh blackberries
- 2 tablespoons granulated sugar
- 1 tablespoon lemon juice
- 1 teaspoon cornstarch

For the Glaze:

- 1 cup powdered sugar
- 2 tablespoons milk
- 1/2 teaspoon vanilla extract

Instructions:

1. Preheat Oven:

- Preheat your oven to 425°F (220°C). Line a baking sheet with parchment paper.

2. Prepare Blackberry Filling:

- In a small saucepan, combine the blackberries, sugar, lemon juice, and cornstarch. Cook over medium heat, stirring occasionally, until the mixture thickens and the blackberries break down. Remove from heat and set aside to cool.

3. Make Biscuit Dough:

- In a large bowl, whisk together the flour, baking powder, baking soda, salt, and sugar.
- Add the cold, diced butter to the dry ingredients. Use a pastry cutter or your fingers to cut the butter into the flour until the mixture resembles coarse crumbs.
- Pour in the buttermilk and vanilla extract. Stir until just combined.

4. Fold in Blackberry Filling:

- Gently fold in the blackberry filling, being careful not to overmix. The dough will be sticky.

5. Form Biscuits:

- Turn the dough out onto a floured surface. Pat it into a rectangle about 1 inch thick.
- Use a round biscuit cutter to cut out biscuits. Place them on the prepared baking sheet, leaving a little space between each.

6. Bake:

- Bake for 12-15 minutes or until the biscuits are golden brown.

7. Prepare Glaze:

- While the biscuits are baking, prepare the glaze by whisking together the powdered sugar, milk, and vanilla extract.

8. Glaze Biscuits:

- Once the biscuits are out of the oven and slightly cooled, drizzle the glaze over the top.

9. Serve:

- Serve the Blackberry Biscuits warm and enjoy!

These blackberry biscuits are a delightful treat, perfect for breakfast or as a sweet snack. The combination of flaky biscuits with a juicy blackberry filling and a sweet glaze is sure to be a hit.

Blackberry Cinnamon Rolls

Ingredients:

For the Dough:

- 4 cups all-purpose flour
- 1/3 cup granulated sugar
- 1 teaspoon salt
- 1 packet (2 1/4 teaspoons) active dry yeast
- 1 1/4 cups warm milk
- 1/4 cup unsalted butter, melted
- 1 large egg

For the Filling:

- 1/2 cup unsalted butter, softened
- 1 cup brown sugar, packed
- 2 tablespoons ground cinnamon
- 1 cup fresh blackberries

For the Cream Cheese Frosting:

- 4 ounces cream cheese, softened
- 1/4 cup unsalted butter, softened
- 2 cups powdered sugar
- 1 teaspoon vanilla extract
- 2-3 tablespoons milk

Instructions:

1. Prepare Dough:

- In a large bowl, combine 3 cups of flour, sugar, and salt. In a separate bowl, dissolve the yeast in warm milk and let it sit for about 5 minutes until it becomes frothy.
- Add the melted butter and egg to the yeast mixture, then add it to the dry ingredients. Mix until a soft dough forms.
- Gradually add the remaining 1 cup of flour until the dough is smooth and elastic.

2. Knead and Rise:

- Turn the dough onto a floured surface and knead for about 5 minutes. Place the dough in a greased bowl, cover it, and let it rise in a warm place for 1-2 hours or until doubled in size.

3. Prepare Filling:

- In a small bowl, mix together the softened butter, brown sugar, and cinnamon to create the filling.

4. Roll and Fill:

- Roll out the risen dough into a large rectangle on a floured surface. Spread the cinnamon-sugar mixture evenly over the dough, then sprinkle fresh blackberries on top.

5. Roll and Cut:

- Starting from one of the long edges, roll the dough into a log. Cut the log into equal-sized rolls.

6. Place in Pan:

- Place the rolls in a greased baking pan, leaving a little space between each.

7. Rise Again:

- Cover the rolls and let them rise for an additional 30-45 minutes.

8. Preheat Oven:

- Preheat your oven to 375°F (190°C).

9. Bake:

- Bake the cinnamon rolls in the preheated oven for 20-25 minutes or until they are golden brown.

10. Make Frosting:

- While the rolls are baking, prepare the cream cheese frosting. Beat together the softened cream cheese, butter, powdered sugar, vanilla extract, and enough milk to achieve a smooth consistency.

11. Frost and Serve:

- Once the rolls are out of the oven, let them cool slightly, then spread the cream cheese frosting over the top.

12. Enjoy:

- Serve the Blackberry Cinnamon Rolls warm and enjoy!

These blackberry cinnamon rolls are a delightful twist on the classic and are sure to be a hit for breakfast or as a sweet treat any time of the day.

Blackberry and Prosciutto Pizza

Ingredients:

For the Pizza Dough:

- 1 pound pizza dough (store-bought or homemade)
- Cornmeal (for dusting)

For the Toppings:

- 1/2 cup pizza sauce
- 1 1/2 cups shredded mozzarella cheese
- 1 cup fresh blackberries
- 4 slices prosciutto
- 1/4 cup crumbled goat cheese
- Fresh arugula (for garnish)
- Balsamic glaze (for drizzling)

Instructions:

1. Preheat Oven:

- Preheat your oven to the temperature recommended for your pizza dough (usually around 450°F or 230°C). If you have a pizza stone, place it in the oven while preheating.

2. Roll Out Pizza Dough:

- Dust a surface with cornmeal and roll out the pizza dough into your desired shape.

3. Assemble the Pizza:

- If using a pizza stone, transfer the rolled-out dough to a piece of parchment paper on a pizza peel or an inverted baking sheet.
- Spread pizza sauce evenly over the dough, leaving a small border for the crust.
- Sprinkle shredded mozzarella over the sauce.
- Distribute fresh blackberries and tear prosciutto slices over the pizza.
- Crumble goat cheese evenly over the top.

4. Bake:

- If using a pizza stone, carefully transfer the parchment paper with the pizza onto the preheated stone in the oven.
- Bake for about 12-15 minutes or until the crust is golden and the cheese is bubbly and slightly browned.

5. Garnish and Serve:

- Remove the pizza from the oven and let it cool for a few minutes.
- Top with fresh arugula and drizzle with balsamic glaze.

6. Slice and Enjoy:

- Slice the pizza into servings and enjoy your Blackberry and Prosciutto Pizza!

This unique pizza combines the sweetness of blackberries with the salty and savory flavors of prosciutto and goat cheese. The addition of fresh arugula and balsamic glaze adds a burst of freshness and tanginess. It's a delightful and sophisticated pizza that's perfect for a special occasion or a gourmet pizza night at home.

Blackberry Trifle

Ingredients:

For the Blackberry Sauce:

- 3 cups fresh blackberries
- 1/3 cup granulated sugar
- 1 tablespoon lemon juice
- 2 tablespoons water
- 1 tablespoon cornstarch

For the Whipped Cream:

- 2 cups heavy cream
- 1/4 cup powdered sugar
- 1 teaspoon vanilla extract

For the Trifle Assembly:

- Pound cake or angel food cake, cut into cubes
- Fresh blackberries for layering
- Mint leaves for garnish (optional)

Instructions:

1. Prepare the Blackberry Sauce:

- In a saucepan, combine the blackberries, sugar, lemon juice, water, and cornstarch.
- Cook over medium heat, stirring frequently until the mixture comes to a simmer and thickens.
- Remove from heat and let it cool. Once cooled, refrigerate until ready to use.

2. Make the Whipped Cream:

- In a chilled mixing bowl, whip the heavy cream until soft peaks form.
- Add powdered sugar and vanilla extract, and continue whipping until stiff peaks form.

3. Assemble the Trifle:

- In a trifle dish or individual serving glasses, start with a layer of cake cubes at the bottom.
- Spoon a layer of the blackberry sauce over the cake cubes.
- Add a layer of fresh blackberries.
- Top with a layer of whipped cream.

4. Repeat Layers:

- Repeat the layers until you reach the top of the trifle dish, finishing with a layer of whipped cream on top.

5. Garnish:

- Garnish the top with additional fresh blackberries and mint leaves if desired.

6. Chill:

- Refrigerate the trifle for at least 2-3 hours or overnight to allow the flavors to meld and the dessert to set.

7. Serve:

- Serve chilled and enjoy this delightful Blackberry Trifle!

This trifle is a perfect summer dessert, showcasing the sweetness of fresh blackberries with layers of cake and velvety whipped cream. It's visually appealing and sure to be a crowd-pleaser at any gathering.

Blackberry and Honey Yogurt Bowl

Ingredients:

- 1 cup Greek yogurt
- 1 cup fresh blackberries
- 2 tablespoons honey
- 1/4 cup granola
- 1 tablespoon chopped nuts (such as almonds or walnuts)
- Fresh mint leaves for garnish (optional)

Instructions:

Prepare the Yogurt Base:
- In a bowl, scoop out the Greek yogurt.

Add Fresh Blackberries:
- Wash and pat dry the blackberries. Add them on top of the Greek yogurt.

Drizzle with Honey:
- Drizzle honey over the yogurt and blackberries. Adjust the amount according to your sweetness preference.

Top with Granola:
- Sprinkle granola over the yogurt and blackberries. This adds a delightful crunch.

Sprinkle Chopped Nuts:
- Add a layer of chopped nuts for additional texture and flavor.

Garnish with Mint Leaves (Optional):
- If you like, garnish the bowl with fresh mint leaves for a burst of freshness.

Serve and Enjoy:
- Mix all the ingredients together just before eating, or enjoy the layers separately. Either way, it's a delicious and nutritious treat.

This Blackberry and Honey Yogurt Bowl is not only visually appealing but also provides a balance of sweetness, tartness, and crunch. It makes for a perfect breakfast or snack, and you can customize it by adding other fruits, seeds, or your favorite toppings.

Blackberry and Peach Sangria

Ingredients:

- 1 bottle of white wine (750 ml), chilled (use your favorite variety)
- 1/2 cup brandy
- 1/4 cup peach schnapps
- 2 tablespoons honey (adjust to taste)
- 1 cup blackberries (fresh or frozen)
- 2 ripe peaches, sliced
- 1 orange, sliced
- 1 lemon, sliced
- 1-2 cups sparkling water or club soda, chilled (adjust to your preference)
- Ice cubes

Instructions:

Prepare the Fruits:
- Wash and slice the peaches, orange, and lemon into thin rounds. Rinse the blackberries.

Combine Ingredients:
- In a large pitcher, combine the chilled white wine, brandy, peach schnapps, and honey. Stir well until the honey is dissolved.

Add Fruits:
- Add the sliced peaches, blackberries, orange slices, and lemon slices to the pitcher. Stir gently to combine.

Chill:
- Place the sangria in the refrigerator and let it chill for at least 2-4 hours, allowing the flavors to meld. You can also leave it overnight for a more infused taste.

Serve:
- Just before serving, add the sparkling water or club soda to the sangria. Adjust the amount based on your desired level of effervescence.

Add Ice:
- Fill glasses with ice cubes and pour the sangria over the ice.

Garnish (Optional):
- Garnish individual glasses with additional blackberries or a slice of peach if desired.

Enjoy:

- Stir the sangria gently in each glass before sipping. Enjoy this fruity and refreshing Blackberry and Peach Sangria!

This sangria is perfect for a sunny day or as a delightful drink for gatherings. The combination of blackberries and peaches adds a sweet and juicy flavor, making it a crowd-pleaser. Adjust the sweetness and alcohol content to suit your taste preferences.

Blackberry Oatmeal Bars

Ingredients:

For the Blackberry Filling:

- 3 cups fresh blackberries
- 1/2 cup granulated sugar
- 2 tablespoons cornstarch
- 1 tablespoon lemon juice

For the Oatmeal Crust and Topping:

- 2 cups old-fashioned oats
- 1 cup all-purpose flour
- 1 cup light brown sugar, packed
- 1/2 teaspoon baking powder
- 1/4 teaspoon salt
- 1 cup unsalted butter, cold and cubed
- 1 teaspoon vanilla extract

Instructions:

1. Preheat the Oven:

- Preheat your oven to 350°F (175°C). Grease a 9x9-inch (23x23 cm) baking pan or line it with parchment paper, leaving an overhang for easy removal.

2. Make the Blackberry Filling:

- In a saucepan, combine the blackberries, sugar, cornstarch, and lemon juice. Cook over medium heat, stirring frequently, until the mixture thickens and the berries break down slightly (about 5-7 minutes). Remove from heat and set aside to cool.

3. Prepare the Oatmeal Crust:

- In a large mixing bowl, combine the oats, flour, brown sugar, baking powder, and salt. Add the cold, cubed butter and vanilla extract. Use a pastry cutter or your hands to combine the ingredients until the mixture resembles coarse crumbs.

4. Assemble the Bars:

- Press about two-thirds of the oat mixture into the bottom of the prepared baking pan to form the crust.
- Spread the blackberry filling evenly over the crust.
- Sprinkle the remaining oat mixture over the blackberry filling, creating a crumbly topping.

5. Bake:

- Bake in the preheated oven for 35-40 minutes or until the top is golden brown and the blackberry filling is bubbly.

6. Cool and Slice:

- Allow the bars to cool completely in the pan on a wire rack. Once cooled, refrigerate for at least 1-2 hours to help set the filling.
- Use the parchment paper overhang to lift the bars out of the pan. Place them on a cutting board and slice into squares.

7. Serve:

- Serve the Blackberry Oatmeal Bars at room temperature and enjoy!

These bars are a delightful combination of sweet, fruity blackberry filling and a buttery oatmeal crust. They make a perfect treat for breakfast, snacks, or dessert. Feel free to customize the recipe with your favorite berries if you like.

Blackberry and Thyme Lemonade

Ingredients:

- 1 cup fresh blackberries
- 1/2 cup granulated sugar (adjust to taste)
- 1 cup fresh lemon juice (about 4-6 lemons)
- 6 cups cold water
- 4-6 sprigs fresh thyme
- Ice cubes
- Lemon slices and blackberries for garnish

Instructions:

1. Make Blackberry Puree:

- In a blender, combine the fresh blackberries and sugar. Blend until you get a smooth puree. If desired, strain the puree through a fine-mesh sieve to remove seeds.

2. Prepare Lemonade Base:

- In a large pitcher, combine the fresh lemon juice and cold water. Stir well to mix.

3. Combine Ingredients:

- Add the blackberry puree to the lemonade base and stir until well combined.

4. Add Thyme:

- Place the fresh thyme sprigs into the pitcher. Gently muddle the thyme with a wooden spoon to release its flavor. You can also leave the thyme sprigs intact for a more subtle thyme infusion.

5. Chill:

- Refrigerate the blackberry and thyme lemonade for at least 1-2 hours to allow the flavors to meld.

6. Serve:

- Fill glasses with ice cubes and pour the chilled blackberry and thyme lemonade over the ice.

7. Garnish:

- Garnish each glass with a slice of lemon and a few fresh blackberries. You can also add a sprig of fresh thyme for an elegant touch.

8. Enjoy:

- Stir the lemonade before drinking to distribute the blackberry flavor evenly. Refresh yourself with this delightful and flavorful Blackberry and Thyme Lemonade!

This homemade lemonade is not only visually appealing with its vibrant color but also offers a perfect balance of sweet blackberry, tart lemon, and aromatic thyme. It's a great drink for warm days or any occasion where you want a tasty and unique beverage.

Blackberry Chocolate Tart

Ingredients:

For the Crust:

- 1 1/2 cups chocolate cookie crumbs (you can use chocolate graham crackers or chocolate wafers)
- 1/3 cup unsalted butter, melted
- 1/4 cup granulated sugar

For the Chocolate Filling:

- 1 1/2 cups dark chocolate, chopped
- 1 cup heavy cream
- 2 tablespoons unsalted butter
- 1 teaspoon vanilla extract

For the Topping:

- 2 cups fresh blackberries
- Powdered sugar for dusting (optional)

Instructions:

1. Prepare the Crust:

- Preheat your oven to 350°F (175°C).
- In a bowl, combine the chocolate cookie crumbs, melted butter, and granulated sugar. Mix until the crumbs are evenly coated.
- Press the mixture into the bottom and up the sides of a tart pan, creating an even crust.
- Bake the crust for about 8-10 minutes, or until set. Allow it to cool completely.

2. Make the Chocolate Filling:

- In a heatproof bowl, combine the chopped dark chocolate, heavy cream, and butter.
- Place the bowl over a pot of simmering water (double boiler) and stir until the chocolate and butter are melted, and the mixture is smooth.

- Remove from heat and stir in the vanilla extract.
- Pour the chocolate filling into the cooled tart crust. Smooth the top with a spatula.
- Place the tart in the refrigerator to set for at least 2 hours, or until the chocolate filling is firm.

3. Add the Blackberry Topping:

- Once the chocolate filling has set, arrange fresh blackberries on top of the tart.
- You can create a pattern or simply scatter them over the chocolate filling.

4. Serve:

- If desired, dust the tart with powdered sugar before serving.
- Slice and enjoy this decadent Blackberry Chocolate Tart!

This tart combines the richness of dark chocolate with the freshness of blackberries, creating a delightful dessert that's perfect for special occasions or whenever you're craving a sweet treat.

Printed in the USA
CPSIA information can be obtained
at www.ICGtesting.com
LVHW061224060924
789972LV00011B/333